PRITCHETT & ASSOCIATES, INC.

Organizations are struggling to speed up. Scrambling to adapt. Trying to innovate, embrace new technologies and respond to a rapidly changing marketplace.

But something's not working.

Word has it that over half of all major change initiatives prove to be disappointments or outright failures.

So what's the problem?

Precious resources are being squandered on organizational civil wars. People are fighting change instead of pushing it forward. They're pulling in different directions rather than aligning with the change efforts.

These are *insiders*. You're paying full dollar for these people. Yet they represent one of the major threats to your organization's future.

Employee resistance is *the* biggest barrier to change.

Let's face it—the very quickest way for the organization to pick up speed is for resisters to take their foot off the brakes. The best way for it to become more adaptive is for people to stop their desperate attempts to preserve the status quo.

The sixteen guidelines in this handbook show you how to free up the valuable energy that's being wasted on resistance. Follow the coaching points given here, because you need the full support of everyone.

PRITCHETT & ASSOCIATES, INC.

Contents

Expect resistance.

Resistance is the most common side effect of change. If you don't encounter it, you have to wonder if you've really changed things much.

Here's how it works.

Change triggers the organization's immune system. People start to resist, trying to fight off the change. It's sort of like antibodies attacking some organism that invades a person's body. This just seems to be the natural order of things. Upset the status quo, and here comes the opposition.

Look at it this way, and you see how resistance *can* be a valuable protective device. For example, strong resistance to change might cause a company to ditch some dangerous new plan or project, just like your body's white blood cells fight off an infection. Resistance can defend the health of organizations as well as individuals.

But resistance also causes problems.

Sometimes even Mother Nature screws up and misdiagnoses a situation. Or tries to defend your body in ways that actually cause trouble. This happens, for example, when the excessive release of histamines causes a person to suffer from hay fever. In much the same way, an *organization's* "body chemistry" can go crazy, such that people do serious damage by resisting changes that are desperately needed.

The main point here is that resistance merely offers evidence that people feel the change. Even if they put up a powerful fight against it, that in itself offers zero proof that the change is wrong. Resistance is a very reliable barometer to measure the *impact* of change. But it's not a good gauge of how *appropriate* the change really is. You can't say change is bad medicine just because some people don't like the taste of it.

You should initiate change with the idea that, more than likely, it will stir up resistance somewhere. Anticipate this, and you're better positioned to handle it.

"Twenty percent of the people will be against anything."
—*Robert Kennedy, U. S. Attorney General*

Remember the "20-50-30 rule."

What sort of push-back is predictable when a major change program gets under way? How much resistance is "reasonable"?

If you have a reliable frame of reference, you can put things into perspective. Knowing what's "normal," you'll have a better feel for how you should react to the particular situation facing you. So let's look at the typical scenario.

We're dealing in generalities here, but the breakout usually goes about like this. Some 20 percent of the people are "change-friendly." They're clear advocates who willingly embrace the change. You can depend on them to help drive the program. Another 50 percent of the folks sit on the fence. They assume a so-called neutral position, trying to figure out which way to lean. They're not necessarily hostile to change, but they're not helping like they should. The remaining 30 percent are the resisters. They're antagonistic toward change and often deliberately try to make it fail.

Guess which group makes the most noise? And who do you think soaks up the most management time and energy?

The resisters, of course. Resistance is seductive stuff. It's hard to ignore. But this is the group that gives you the least return on the efforts you invest. And giving resisters your attention often just *reinforces* their problem behavior. It's sort of like giving media attention to a small band of protesters who are demonstrating. They love it when they make the evening news, and become even more determined in defending their cause.

It makes more sense to spend your time trying to woo the fence-sitters. You have far better odds of winning them over. You also should devote generous attention to the 20 percent who are driving the change. They deserve it the most, but ordinarily they're taken for granted.

Romancing the resisters, to a large extent, is a distraction. Sure, you can put the change effort on hold, and focus on turning these people around. But how long will that take? Can you actually pull it off? And is it even essential?

Really what you're after are *hard results*, rather than getting people to feel happy about what's going on. Never presume that you must have buy-in from everyone before you move forward. For a good percentage of people, buy-in will only come later—if at all—after the results are in which prove that the change was both appropriate and successful.

You must be willing to let squeaky wheels squeak. Save your grease for the quieter wheels that are actually carrying the load.

> *"The secret of managing is to keep the guys who hate you away from the guys who are undecided."*
> — Casey Stengel

Explain the rationale for change.

Resistance often is rooted in a lack of understanding. People withhold support simply because they haven't figured out the situation.

Education is the first step in helping everybody get with the program. Give them the logic that's driving the change. Build your case, and make it compelling. Portray the situation as a crisis, if possible, so people come to the conclusion that *some* kind of change is absolutely necessary.

Your explanation should widen their field of vision. Relate the situation to trends in your industry. Show how your organization measures up against performance benchmarks. Try to relate the proposed changes to your organization's core values. And always consider the situation from your audience's perspective, because it needs to make sense from where *they* sit.

Granted, some people won't accept the party line. But you want everyone to understand it. *Completely.* Then at least nobody can plead ignorance. Or excuse their opposition to the change on the grounds of being uninformed. Or blame somebody else for their own resistive behavior.

Communicating the "why" behind change won't get rid of all resistance. Some folks will refuse to buy your logic. Some others who do accept your rationale will resist anyway because they don't like how they're affected by the change. But leaving people in the dark is just asking for trouble. Explain specifically why change is under way—making sure your rationale holds together—and more people are likely to get on board.

Never assume everybody automatically catches on, even if the reasons for change should be obvious. Spell it out for them. And don't expect people to "get it" just because you've explained it once or twice. Some folks are slow learners—maybe they're not paying attention, maybe they're just hard to convince.

You need to keep at it until everyone knows where the change is coming from. Without that, it's hard to hold people accountable for their behavior.

"This taught me a lesson, but I'm not sure what it is."
— John McEnroe, on losing to Tim Mayotte in the Ebel U. S. Pro Indoor Championships

Choose your opening moves carefully.

Change makes enemies very easily. And the way you *begin* a change effort determines what kind of fight is coming.

Some people choose the subtle approach. The strategy here is to slip in under the enemy radar, to change things quietly and gradually without arousing opposition. If people aren't paying close attention, they probably won't catch on. The question is, how big a step can you take without tipping your hand?

In today's world you really don't have the time needed to follow this strategy. Sure, if you could afford to inch along, and if you have the patience, this low-keyed approach would be the least traumatic. Plus, it's particularly appealing if you don't like conflict. But the slow and subtle approach, if detected, is easily countered. Resisters rally quickly. They'll scramble, start recruiting others to help them fight, and overpower your change initiative with a more aggressive battle plan.

Gradual change may look like the safest route, but appearances are deceptive. Going slow is usually a big gamble.

If you're going to make major changes, the opposite approach offers a lot more promise. Big change calls for bold strokes. Your opening moves need to be dramatic. You need to hit hard...shatter the status quo...shock the organization. The impact should be powerful enough to overcome inertia. When you play this angle you *want* to get people's attention. Instead of trying to sneak past any resistance to change, you come on so strong you scare off the opposition. Or at least you gain the advantage because your opening moves give you a big head start on the resisters. Plus, you send a very convincing message about your determination to make change stick.

The third and least promising way to begin is with the middle-of-the-road approach. It's the most common, but the least effective. Basically it amounts to muddling along—being neither subtle, nor bold and dramatic. It offers none of the benefits of the other two strategies. The enemies of change find it the easiest to resist. They see what's coming, and the sight of that mainly serves to mobilize their counter-attack.

The bottom line is that opening moves are crucial. The way you start a change effort says a lot about how you'll finish.

"It's not a matter of life and death.
It's more important than that."
— *Lou Duva, on the upcoming fight of his protege*
against boxer Mike Tyson.

Provide a clear aiming point.

Resistance to change climbs fast when people can't figure out where they're headed. The more vague the destination, the fewer volunteers you'll find eager to go there.

Keep in mind the fact that change, in general, causes some folks to lose their nerve. No reason why you should contribute to this problem. Since ambiguity leads to uncertainty, you should do what you can to give people a clear sense of direction.

If the organization is drifting and goals are blurry, employees become more tentative. That translates into low-voltage resistance. People start to pull back. They drag their feet. Naturally, organizational change bogs down.

A well defined aiming point helps everyone navigate through the usual mess and confusion. Provide a clear map—a picture of the future that's easy to read and understand—and people are less likely to feel lost or adrift. Even when change becomes scary, frustrating, and downright hard work, clear goals help keep people from giving up.

A goal gives hope—a good antidote to fear—and that reduces resistance. Even people who don't find the goal particularly appealing will show less resistance than if the future is left fuzzy and vague.

Ideally, though, you should make the aiming point desirable, so it has a powerful magnetic pull. The more the future seems forbidding, the more people are likely to resist change. A dangerous looking tomorrow causes people to romanticize the past and protect the status quo. After all, who wants to climb over a mountain of problems unless there's a "promised land" on the other side? Aimless misery is hard to sell.

Make your change goals easy to see, and identify an end point that makes the struggle of change worthwhile. Change needs to be *purposeful* for people to commit.

"They spend their time mostly looking forward to the past."
— *John Osborne in* Look Back in Anger

Take care of the "me" issues.

You can't expect people to be gung-ho about change when they can't even figure out how it's going to affect them. Call it self-preservation, or just good common sense. They want to know, "What's going to happen to *me?*"

More specifically, the "me" issues sound like this: "Will I still have a job?...What will I be doing?...Who will I report to?...Will my pay or benefits be affected?" And so on.

Human beings just have this hang-up: They worry about old number one.

People naturally want answers, particularly when they feel threatened and vulnerable. And they deserve to know what's in store for them personally. Even if they're in line for some bad news, stalling never seems to help the situation.

Most folks find that the toughest thing to deal with is *not knowing*. Starving for answers. Living in an information vacuum. People instinctively start to resist change when they can't draw a bead on what's about to happen to them. This is why "stonewalling" doesn't work worth a hoot as a strategy for minimizing resistance to change. It simply adds to the problem.

The sooner you get rid of the question marks people are carrying around in their minds, the sooner they're in a position to support organizational change. What's interesting is how getting *closure* helps people get past resistance, even when change obviously isn't going to work in their best interests.

The most promising approach is to resolve the "me" issues as quickly as possible, even when it means telling people what they don't want to hear. Sooner is better than later. In those cases where you can't give people what they want, the way you give them what they *don't want* is more important than ever.

"There's nothing I'm afraid
of like scared people."
— Robert Frost

Seek opportunities to involve your people.

Most of us accept change better if we don't think it's being crammed down our throats. We'd rather have a chance to chew on it for a while, even if we eventually have to swallow it.

This is a good argument for giving people an active role in designing how change will unfold. For one thing, they don't feel so helpless. If they can have a voice in matters that directly affect them, they don't feel so vulnerable. Maybe they won't have a knee jerk reaction and instinctively resist.

Another benefit of involving people comes in their having to struggle with the complicated aspects of the situation. They learn a lot. For example, they find out that there are no perfect solutions. When they have to wrestle with the hairy problems themselves, they develop a greater respect for the difficulties involved. This new level of understanding leaves them less blameful. Less critical of the final solution. After all, if they were one of the architects, they're less entitled to complain about having to live in the building.

But the advantages of involving your people can go beyond developing broader support for the change effort. With more minds working on it, you might actually come up with a better strategy than you'd design by yourself.

Now for the bad news.

All this participation sounds good in theory, but it can be a nightmare in practice. You need to know the pros and cons, and weigh them carefully.

Here are the negatives. The more people you get involved, the more you're likely to slow things down. "Change by committee" gets clumsy.

Group-think often dilutes the quality of decisions, too, resulting in watered-down efforts. You can end up with a change program that's popular, but poorly conceived.

Ask yourself at the very outset if your people should have any say-so at all in deciding *whether* to make the change, or just in *how to carry it out*. Or should they have a voice in either one? Inviting them to give input might just complicate the process, causing resistance to come faster and hit harder.

This is one of those tough judgment calls. Involving your people is great when it works. Just remember you're playing with a two-edged sword.

"Don't pay any attention to the critics—don't even ignore them."
— Samuel Goldwyn, movie mogul

Promise problems.

Change produces some rather nasty side effects. The intent is to "fix things," but the actual payoff frequently comes as a delayed reaction. You set out to make things better, but before you get very far you have to deal with the problems of your solutions.

This is the "it gets worse before it gets better" phenomenon. And it's totally predictable.

As people have to break their familiar routines, performance weakens. It's an awkward time, with more confusion, communication problems and job stress.

This is a completely normal turn of events. Just the same, it looks bad. If people aren't mentally prepared for it, chances are they'll conclude that the plan isn't working. The grumbling gets louder, and the change effort loses steam.

Resistance always spikes up when the predictable problems of change take people by surprise. So you need to set the stage. Make it clear at the very outset that change won't be a trouble-free process.

Sure, you should make a sales pitch for the change. Just be sure to point out the warning label as well.

The big mistake is to paint only the rosy part of the picture, limiting your forecasting to some song and dance about how great the change is going to be. That kind of propaganda will come back to haunt you. The fact is, not everything will be just fine and dandy. Problems always crop up when serious change gets under way. If you come across as a Pollyanna, you'll kill your credibility, your people will be resentful, and they'll be less likely to support you going forward. It's not pretty.

The best move is to give everyone an accurate sense of what's coming. This amounts to a balancing act, where you mix the good news with the bad. If you level with them, then at least they can steel themselves for the struggle ahead.

John Sununu (then governor of New Hampshire):

"You're telling us that the reason things are so bad is that they are so good, and they will get better as soon as they get worse?"

James A. Baker (then Secretary of the Treasury):

"You got it."

Over-communicate.

Somebody once said, "The more unpleasant the message, the more effort should go into communicating it." This point is worth keeping in mind as you're trying to push change.

Most major change initiatives run into public relations problems rather quickly. People see and hear things that disturb them. They're disappointed by all the problems...that always seem to arrive well ahead of the successes. As usual, bad news drives good news away, so people disregard much of that which actually represents progress.

Communication is *the* crucial element in keeping the program moving.

As people increasingly question the need for change, you must remind them of the logic behind the effort. When they complain about all the problems, you need to showcase the benefits. If they begin to lose heart, you should offer words that help them keep the faith.

Your job is to be a promoter. An encourager. Change requires lots of cheerleading, and you need to do it loud enough to be heard above all the noise from the critics and naysayers.

Still, not all of your communication efforts need a positive spin. Some information should be passed along to your people in a matter-of-fact manner, without any rah-rah. For example, they need general updates on a frequent basis. It's even smart to keep them posted about problems, and to advise them of bad news well in advance.

Also, do your best to make communication a two-way street. Ask questions. Listen. Create completely new channels that make it easy and safe for people to express themselves.

Change just naturally creates an information vacuum, an atmosphere where there are more questions than answers. If you fail to satisfy your people's craving for communication, the rumor mill will fill the void. That leads to worst-case thinking, a lot of warped messages, and an overheated worry factor that gets in the way of work.

Granted, good communication takes a lot of time and effort. But it's a great investment. You'll find a direct correlation between the quality of communication and how much resistance comes your way.

"Last night I neglected to mention something that bears repeating."
— Ron Fairly, San Francisco Giants broadcaster, during on-air game coverage.

Beware of bureaucracy.

Large or small, profit or not-for-profit, public or private—*every* organization has its own bureaucracy...its red tape...its cadre of bureaucrats. This is "the System," the "Establishment."

And this is the enemy of change.

Bureaucracy's primary virtue lies in its ability to stabilize things. It provides structure. Routine. Role clarity and predictability. Obviously, that has value. But bureaucracy has a habit of reproducing itself, eventually clogging the organization with too much of a good thing. It causes work patterns to stiffen and become inflexible routines. It lets once-serviceable guidelines deteriorate into procedural ruts. Its emphasis on petty rules and proper forms stifles innovation and interferes with change.

Bureaucracy actually legitimizes resistance. All of that stability sought and supported by the bureaucrats is incompatible with change's constant companions: ambiguity and uncertainty, confusion, renegotiation of power, shifting roles and responsibilities. You need to know that, in the struggle that develops, bureaucracy fights dirty.

The bureaucrats rely heavily on covert tactics. Passive resistance is their forte. For example, riding the fence rather than taking a clear position. Dragging their feet. Rationalizing the need to "go slow and avoid mistakes." Waging their own private turf battles by means of red tape and standard operating procedures. Circulating behind the scenes to spread doubt and sabotage the game plan for change.

They're good at it. They're so good, in fact, that they always prolong the change process. Some change initiatives manage to stumble along in spite of bureaucracy's counteroffensive. But far too many programs just die a slow death. Usually, if the bureaucrats prevail with their warnings to "go slow," they buy enough time to fend off the changes or at least blunt the effort.

You can expect the bureaucrats to wrap themselves in the corporate flag and warn that the change is ill-conceived. Maybe unnecessary. Likely as not, these prophets of doom believe their own propaganda. Bureaucrats can be well intentioned in their efforts to "protect" the organization against itself. But even if you give them the benefit of the doubt as to their motivation, you must dismiss their rhetoric. And you must override their argument for preserving the status quo. In "defending" the organization, they're protecting what "used to be" instead of what "needs to be."

Frankly, you won't have much luck *selling* change to these people. So just go ahead anyway. Make it happen. You might as well accept the fact that you can't successfully implement major change and keep the bureaucrats happy. You have to push them kicking and screaming into tomorrow.

Above all, do not underestimate the enemy. Bureaucracy looks at all this as a life or death struggle. So meet the beast head-on.

"I hate being a bureaucrat and will resign as soon as I know the proper procedures."
— *Cartoon caption by Hector Breeze*

Wear your commitment on your sleeve.

A lot of resistance dies out once people come to the conclusion that change is a done deal. If they can tell that you're not just testing the water, that there truly is no going back, opposition quickly tapers off.

By the same token, it takes precious little to keep hope alive in the hearts of resisters. And they're relentlessly searching for any shred of evidence to help them believe the change effort might be aborted. You can *say* change is for keeps, but that falls way short of making them believers. Frankly, your words will count for little until they are backed up by tangible evidence that you mean what you say.

People will "test the limits," looking to find their own proof of how serious you are about this. You must be resolute. Once you've weighed the alternatives, given others a chance for input, and settled on the best course of action, never waiver in your resolve. Be obvious—and passionate—in your determination to follow through.

The fight will intensify as your opposition pushes back, challenging the change, and checking to see if you'll hold your ground. Don't let this take you by surprise. Just handle it.

Don't try to reduce the resistance by softening your position. It will only *stiffen* the resistance. This is a situation that calls for some true rigidity on your part.

Again, actions speak louder than words. This is where you may need to make an example out of someone who resists. If so, it should be a high profile action. Make it very public. The idea is for many people to get the message—*it's time to get on board.*

During major change, you've got to be willing to have some significant fallout. Some casualties. If this sounds ruthless, just remember— the resisters consciously choose their behavior. They're adults. They know what they're doing. Something has to suffer, either them or your change effort.

"The people who change best and fastest are the ones who have no choice."
— *Robert Frey, in* Harvard Business Review

Alter the reward system to support change.

Picture this: An organization asks people to change, then rewards them better if they stay the same.

Makes no sense whatsoever, but it happens all the time. Basically it comes down to this—*people get paid to resist.*

This is the absurd situation that develops when we ask people to change their behavior, but fail to make it worth their while. They usually decide to keep doing the same old things instead. And why not? It's probably easier. Maybe it seems less risky. But most important, it offers a better payoff than changing does.

Think about it. People often stand to lose somehow in the change process. Work gets harder, at least for a while. There's more job stress. Overall, the personal costs seem rather high. If resisting change doesn't cause them problems, then why worry about changing? Hanging on to old habits makes pretty good sense, so long as the old reward system stays in place.

You must give people eye-catching reasons to do things differently. If you want them to align with the organization as it moves in new directions, then make it a paying proposition.

Restructure the way people get compensated. Tie base pay, raises and bonuses to the behavior shifts that are needed to support the change. Reserve promotions and the most sought after assignments for the people who do the most to drive change forward. Pass out "psychological paychecks"—praise, attention, honors or awards—in a more discriminating manner, rewarding only those people who get with the program.

Then consider the steps you need to take with *negative* reinforcement. Just as you need to offer everybody a powerful new payoff for *supporting* change, you also need to make it expensive for them if they *fight* it. Resistance should produce a more unpleasant set of results than change does. Sticking with the status quo needs to be a painful, unsatisfying experience.

These are common sense ideas, but they're not commonly considered when change efforts are being engineered. As a result, people end up with little immediate incentive to change. So they don't. Or to put it differently, they resist.

You *must* alter the way rewards work in the system, or you can expect more or less the same behavior you've been seeing.

"Don't forget, folks—the less you bet, the more you lose when you win."
— advice from a stickman at the
Landmark Casino, Las Vegas

Get resistance out into the open.

Resistance should be hunted down. Understood. Taken seriously. The more it remains a mystery, and the more you minimize it, the more vulnerable your change effort becomes.

Some of the resistance problems you can't miss. Category 1 resisters *try* to call attention to themselves. They're loud, outspoken, very high profile in their opposition to change. These firebrands or rabble-rousers create the highest noise level, but usually are one of the smallest groups of resisters. Category 2 is less obvious, but larger. These are the moderates. People in this group aren't so brazen, and some deliberately disguise their resistance to make it safer or politically correct. But Category 3 people are the most cunning of all. They operate under cover, resisting on the sly, fighting change oh-so-carefully to minimize their chances of being caught. These are the saboteurs, the silent enemies of change. If the firebrands rely on frontal assault, Category 3 resisters prefer the sneak attack. Guerrilla warfare. Who knows how large this group really is.

People in all three groups can cause you big problems, but you have to handle them differently. In dealing with the firebrands, finding them isn't the problem. Understanding them is. You have to get beyond the hostility and the high decibel level, because only then do you discover what's *really* causing all the fireworks. You also have to turn your back to some of the racket. A lot of it is just noise pollution, and it will distract you from what's going on with the other resisters.

Moderates can be approached in a fairly straightforward manner. But watch for resistance that may be masquerading as something else.

As for the saboteurs, your job is to blow their cover. Look for signs of *passive* resistance—for example, foot dragging, quiet uncooperativeness, deliberately letting things slip through the cracks, malicious compliance, etc. When you spot this behavior, corner the people and get them talking.

Always make it safe and easy for people to open up. Be patient enough to get beyond superficial answers so you reach the true issues. The reasons for resistance can run extremely deep, and you really need to get to the heart of the matter. Otherwise you'll end up attacking the wrong problems.

Operate from the premise that people resist for what they consider to be good reasons. Try to understand their position. Evaluate the legitimacy of their resistance. You might even discover that some of them are more like allies than adversaries. They can round out your perspective...position you to do better decision-making...keep you from doing something dumb that's doomed to fail. At the very least they can educate you about why they're resisting and how you might elicit their support.

You gain a lot just by showing respect for the resisters and treating them with dignity. That alone might keep resistance from escalating. Discounting their perspective generally gives them the feeling they must fight the change more aggressively. And disallowing resistance altogether usually just drives it underground. You don't want that. When resistance disappears from view, it's more dangerous than ever.

"The conventional army loses if it does not win. The guerrilla wins if he does not lose."
— *Henry Kissinger*

Make sure people have the know-how needed.

Question: What do most people do when they don't know what to do?

Think about that for a minute. Then think about how often organizations introduce change, but leave people clueless about how to proceed. This is one of the most chronic mistakes in change management.

We have a bad habit of overlooking the knowledge gap that change creates. People have to handle new kinds of equipment. They face unfamiliar methodologies. There might be a new boss, a different mix of coworkers, or culture changes to accommodate. There's an awful lot to learn. There's also the problem of unclear expectations—people wonder what to stop doing...what to start doing, and how...what to keep on doing, but differently.

Who's likely to tear into *that* with confidence and enthusiasm? Wouldn't *you* resist?

Higher management plans a change crusade and says, "Charge!" But the foot soldiers don't know how to fire their weapons. The marching orders are delivered forcefully, but the people can't figure out how to fight. Should we be surprised when they don't attack?

What looks like obstinance or lack of cooperation on the part of your people may prove to be a simple lack of know-how. On the surface it can seem like they're resisting change. But maybe they'd just rather do nothing than do wrong. It's easy to see how people might freeze up because they're afraid of failure.

If they feel trapped in a situation that's dangerous, different and vague, you should help them develop the new skills they need. If they're afraid of becoming obsolete—worrying whether they'll ever be competent again—you should retrain them for new jobs.

Invest heavily in front-end education, and your change effort will come off the line much faster. Train...coach...school your people. Show them how to succeed in the new scheme of things.

If you expect people to perform differently, make sure they know how to go about it.

"Nothing made sense and neither did everything else."
— *Joseph Heller*

Track behavior and measure results.

Major change efforts require constant monitoring. Things go wrong. Unexpected situations develop. Even the most carefully planned change strategy will need occasional fine tuning. And *resistance* will serve as one of your best diagnostic tools.

You'll find some resistance is due to the fact that certain aspects of the game plan for change were wrong to begin with. Or maybe that they're being carried out poorly. Resistance, in this sense, is actually beneficial. If you're paying attention, it signals problems or mistakes, and gives you a chance to re-calibrate your approach.

Most of the time, though, resistance is an enemy. You need to know where it hides, who's energizing it, and what kind of damage it's doing. Otherwise, resistance has you at its mercy.

You must be alert, vigilant, always on the lookout for the tracks it leaves. You're dealing with a moving target here, so you should be constantly scanning. If you're watchful enough, you'll catch resistance red-handed. So circulate. Talk to people. Above all, track results. Look for symptoms like slippages in timetables. Productivity downturns. Weakening sales figures. Other obvious signs are uncooperativeness, complaining and criticizing the people in charge.

Resistance can be overt or covert. Active or passive. Well-intentioned or subversive. People fight change in ways that best fit their individual personalities, so you'll detect a wide range of tactics at work.

A few folks will be innocent enough in their intent—maybe even oblivious to the fact that their behavior is a problem. Resistance can occur if people get confused, drift off course, or just quite naturally start regressing to the old way of doing things. If you're paying attention, you can address the problem before it gets out of hand.

Keep in mind that resistance comes and goes. Sometimes there's trouble everywhere, and you're in a firefighting mode. Then there'll be quiet spells, where it's tempting to relax and let down your guard. But don't do it. Get complacent, and the next thing you know the change program will be wrapped around the axle somewhere. There are several stages to any major change initiative. Resistance has a way of erupting suddenly when the change reaches a new set of people.

Finally, one last reason for monitoring performance and tracking results: It enables you to identify the new heroes, the role models who are contributing the most to the change effort. You need to single these people out...honor them...and celebrate their achievements.

"What gets measured becomes important."
—Unknown

Outrun the resisters.

Resisters rely on a strategy of delay. Naturally, speed is the adversary they fear the most. They *hate* "fast."

Actually, the resisters don't really even want "slow"...they want "not at all." "Slow" is just the argument they use to get there. Their behavior is carefully calculated to make the change process stall.

Resisters wag their heads and warn about the risks of rapid change. They condemn speed as reckless, shaming those who are in favor of quick execution. They want to sit down...talk things over...weigh the risks again... consider other options... ruminate over what might possibly go wrong. You'll hear them emphasize the value of deliberation. They lobby hard for not making mistakes. They can present a powerful case—appealing to "reason," and doing a guilt trip on you with their holier-than-thou attitude.

Be careful, or the resisters will con you into making the most fundamental mistake of all: Letting them choose the pace of change. Agreeing to go slow gives them home field advantage. Or even worse, it's like letting the opponent call all your plays. Is this a game you can win?

Careful deliberation is appropriate in the planning stage, when you're trying to decide on the right course of action. But even there resisters can bog things down in analysis-paralysis and indecision. In today's high-velocity world, you should push for prompt, crisp decision-making. And once you start to implement, you should execute at a blistering pace. The quicker the change effort gains momentum, the harder it is to stop.

The idea is to keep the opposition off balance. Force the resisters to play catch up. Make change happen in a hurry—*get it done*—such that resistance hardly serves any purpose.

If your conscience starts to bother you because of all the criticism, consider this: The resisters talk one game, but walk another. They want the proponents of change to go slow, yet they personally *resist* fast. Ask yourself, did they actually deliberate about the best course of action, carefully weighing the pros and cons of resisting? Have they taken the time to truly think through the ramifications of their opposition? No. They don't play by the rules they argue for. Resistance is typically a reckless, impulsive act. And usually it's based on quite selfish motives.

The fact is, in today's fiercely competitive marketplace, slow change doesn't have a very high success rate. Quite the opposite. Slow *raises* the risk factor. There are far more failures from going too slowly than from exceeding some imaginary speed limit.

"It gets late early out there."
— *Yogi Berra*

In Closing...

Let's end with where you should begin—with the focus on *your* reaction to change.

Day in, day out, what sort of example do you set? Are you personally a role model for adaptability? Do you lead others into change... or do you somehow lead them into resistance?

Consider how many people take their cue from you. Ask yourself what kind of influence you carry. And when change hits, remember to move yourself first, so you don't get in the way of others.

—*Price Pritchett*

ORDER FORM

Resistance:
Moving Beyond the Barriers to Change

1-99 copies	____ copies at 5.95 each
100-999 copies	____ copies at 5.75 each
1,000-4,999 copies	____ copies at 5.50 each
5,000-9,999 copies	____ copies at 5.25 each
10,000 or more copies	____ copies at 5.00 each

> To place orders, call toll free **800-992-5922**
> or drop your order in the mail using this order form.
> Orders may be faxed to **214-789-7900**.

Name _____

Job Title _____

Organization _____

Phone _____

Street Address _____ Zip _____

P.O. Box _____ Zip _____

City, State _____

Country _____

Purchase order number (if applicable) _____

Applicable sales tax, shipping and handling charges will be added. Prices subject to change.

Orders less than $100 require prepayment. $100 or more may be invoiced.

☐ Check Enclosed   ☐ Please Invoice

☐ **VISA**   ☐ **MasterCard**   ☐ **AMERICAN EXPRESS**

Account Number _____ Expiration Date _____

Signature _____

800-992-5922
Overnight or Second Day Deliveries
Available via Federal Express or UPS.

PRITCHETT & ASSOCIATES, INC.
13155 Noel Road, Suite 1600, Dallas, Texas 75240
214-789-7999 • FAX 214-789-7900

95783

Management Consulting Services

Pritchett & Associates developed its in-depth expertise by working with Fortune 500 clients for over 20 years. The key to our success is an intimate understanding of organizations undergoing major change—we combine extensive, "hands-on" executive experience with an analytic, results-oriented approach to problem solving. Our consultants have the know-how to:

- Exploit instability rather than merely cope with change.
- Assess your culture, organization, and management processes to develop high-impact change initiatives.
- Move you from plans to accomplishments...to become an adaptive organization.
- Apply leading edge change management expertise and merger integration services to your critical business challenges.

Training Programs to Implement Change

Pritchett training programs build on the hard-hitting principles in our best-selling handbooks. These quick-impact, concentrated programs have been successfully used by organizations worldwide. They deliver a no-nonsense message on how to deal with today's rapidly changing business environment. Our training will help your organization:

- Recognize the predictable dynamics of change.
- Convert "change resisters" to "change agents."
- Improve operating effectiveness and productivity during change.
- Shorten the high-risk transition period.
- Keep people focused on the "high priority" issues.
- Restore stability and morale.

BOOKS BY PRITCHETT & ASSOCIATES, INC.

The Ethics of Excellence

*The Employee Survival Guide to Mergers
   and Acquisitions*

After the Merger: Managing the Shockwaves

*Making Mergers Work: A Guide to
   Managing Mergers and Acquisitions*

* *Service Excellence!*

* *Business As UnUsual: The Handbook for
   Managing and Supervising Organizational
   Change*

* *The Employee Handbook for Organizational
   Change*

* *Team ReConstruction: Building A High
   Performance Work Group During Change*

* *High-Velocity Culture Change: A Handbook
   for Managers*

*Smart Moves: A Crash Course on Merger
   Integration Management*

** Training program also available.
Please call 1-800-622-8989 for
more information.*

*Call 214-789-7999 for information
regarding international rights and
foreign translations.*

Price Pritchett is Chairman and CEO of Pritchett & Associates, Inc., a Dallas-based firm specializing in mergers and organizational change. He has authored 19 books on individual and organizational performance, and is recognized internationally as a leading authority on the dynamics of change. He holds a Ph.D. in psychology and has consulted to top executives in major corporations for two decades.

PRITCHETT & ASSOCIATES, INC.